MY JOURNEY
TO THE
NEXT WORLD

By

COREY LAFFERTY

With

Jane Dobry

MY JOURNEY

TO THE

NEXT WORLD

ISBN: 978-0-692-35578-7

Cover Illustration by Corey Lafferty

Acknowledgements

I'd like to express my deepest appreciation to my mother, Sharon Colombo Lafferty, who assisted in my endeavor to write this book. In her diligence, she purchased all the medical records and preserved all the accounts and events which took place during and after my hospital stay through a detailed journal. She also submitted my after-death experience to the *Near Death Experience Research Foundation*; which determined my recollections as authentic. I'd also like to acknowledge the efforts of Marianne (Jane) Lafferty, my grandmother, who weaved together all the documents and first-hand accounts into a story; and Raymond (Ralph) Lafferty, my grandfather, for his technical support. I'd also like to add a very special thank you to all of the medical people who have been a part of my care at Mott Children's Hospital, St. John Hospital and DMC's Children's Hospital.

A Sunday Afternoon on the Island of La Grande Jatte - 1884

French - Georges-Pierre Seurat, 1859-1891

You only live twice.
Once when you are born,
Once when you look death in the face;

..................."and Heaven sends you back."

Ian Fleming

haiku, written in the style of
Japanese poet Matsuo Basho

Revision by Corey Lafferty

There is always hope, even in the deepest parts of despair. If you feel that you've lost all hope, remember this story of a young boy who changed everything in his life for the better; because he never lost hope, and never will.

Corey Lafferty

The Road Not Taken

Robert Frost, 1874 - 1963

Two roads diverged in a yellow wood,
And sorry I could not travel both
And be one traveler, long I stood
And looked down one as far as I could
To where it bent in the undergrowth;

Then took the other, as just as fair,
And having perhaps the better claim,
Because it was grassy and wanted wear;
Though as for that the passing there
Had worn them really about the same,

And both that morning equally lay
In leaves no step had trodden black.
Oh, I kept the first for another day!
Yet knowing how way leads on to way,
I doubted if I should ever come back.

I shall be telling this with a sigh
Somewhere ages and ages hence:
Two roads diverged in a wood, and I--
I took the one less traveled by,
And that has made all the difference.

Dedication

I would like to dedicate this book to my parents, Sharon and Michael Lafferty, my two siblings, Erik and Lily, and to every other member of my family including Jane Dobry who helped me write this book. I especially want to thank my amazing friends: Syed Ali, Natalie Kedrow (Campbell), Alex Henry, Wakhiel Moshon, Racheal Robbins, Shaun-Patrick Allen, Elijsha Baetiong, and Mahir Chowdhury, who walked with me on this journey, and to all of those who supported me through the years after the accident. Also, I extend my deepest gratitude to the "Great Illustrator" Mark Crilley, who has inspired me for so many years and will continue to do so for the anticipated years to come.

Table of Contents   Page

June 23, 2007

It was a tremendous decision for a ten year old boy to make. Did I want to remain in the majesty and glory of Heaven, Jesus asked, or did I want to return to my life on Earth? The choice was mine. I so wanted to stay. The love and compassion emanating from Jesus was compelling and more abundant than any emotion I'd ever experienced in my short earthly life. He was unlike any portrait or picture I'd ever seen. I can only explain that I understood the power of Jesus as I felt His presence and intense love.

I also knew I was with God. She was greater than anything and everything beyond human comprehension. She was the entity I had always known; for I was the core of Her Being just as She was the core of mine. To explain this familiarity in language is impossible.

All words are totally and completely inadequate. My visit with Her in Heaven was an experience unlike any human sense because it was more authentic than any human sense. God was more radiant than the sun, but with a calming brilliance. I could look at Her with ease, as I never dared look at the sun. Gazing upon Her gentle splendor, I was one with God.

Corey Lafferty

The Journey

I don't remember anything about the day I drowned. I don't even remember the days leading up to that fateful trip which resulted in a dramatic life-change not just for me, but for my family. My mother, Sharon, was taking my sister Lily and my brother Erik and I to a lakeside cabin in Alpena, Michigan. Both of my siblings were older than I. Lily had just turned fourteen and Erik was eleven. We lived in Warren; just outside of Detroit and the drive north along Michigan's eastern coast would take about four hours. The cabin was on a beach next to Lake Huron, one of Michigan's Great Lakes.

My father, Michael Lafferty, did not want us to go without him. He had just returned home after a brief U.S. and Canadian tour with the band, Uncle Kracker. My dad was a known local musician in a band called Rockstar. He is an excellent keyboardist and vocalist. He also plays the guitar and other instruments. He was also a Quality Manager working for MagnaChek during the day. These responsibilities precluded him from joining us that weekend but would not interfere with our planned trip to Disneyworld in two months. It was one of Dad's favorite places to visit and this time, Mom's sisters and their families would be meeting us there. My mother, Sharon, was looking forward to some time away from her job as the head of the Nuclear Medicine Department at St. John Macomb Hospital. She loved her work and was always continuing her education. Dad's parents thought Mom should have been a medical doctor. They saw that as her true vocation.

Up until that June day in 2007, my life was pretty normal. Of course I fought with Lily and Erik over all sorts of real or imagined injustices, but I always loved my sister and brother. There was never any doubt that our parents loved us too although we could be trying at times. We also spent a lot of time with Nana and Poppy, Dad's parents. They helped raise us. Busia was Nana's mother, so they brought her to live with them after Dziadek died.

I still remember Nana's father, Dziadek, (Jah-dek) so very well. He used to like to play games with me and I always accused him of cheating. I would tell him he was in "big trouble." That always seemed to amuse him but I didn't know why. I'd tell on him to Busia but Nana would explain that Dziadek really didn't know the rules of the new games I would bring him. That was true only to a point. Dziadek certainly knew how to play checkers! Dziadek also liked to play the lottery. Every day he would play the numbers 643. Those numbers were part of his Social Security Number and I guess he thought they were lucky. They weren't. Busia said he should have given her a dollar a day instead of spending it on a lottery ticket. She'd have saved more than he'd ever won. That combination of numbers lived on even after he died though, and brought comfort to Nana throughout the coming years. When she would see 643, she knew Dziadek was still taking care of his family from another realm.

The day before we left, Busia warned us to be especially careful when we were in the water, for she was always afraid of it. Dziadek always said that a person who respects a body of water and recognizes its power need not fear it. Poppy told us to stay near the shore and so did Nana.

Dad decided he would drive the morning of our departure from our home in Warren to Frankenmuth, a popular tourist destination known for its German ancestry and chicken dinners. We would all arrive together and he would have breakfast with us at Tony's, a restaurant known for its huge servings of food. He would then head back to Warren and we'd make our way north to Alpena. During our meal, Mom talked about the dream she'd had the night before.   It caused her some distress. It contributed to my father's sense of foreboding.

Mom relayed the dream to us. It was about her parents. The memory of Grandpa and Grandma's untimely deaths that year within months of each other was painfully with us and the dream compounded our sadness.   While dreaming, Mom was in her parents' house with her three older siblings; the twins, Mary and Sue and her other sister, Karen.   Even though Mom loved being with her entire family again, she woke from the dream crying.   It left her feeling anxious.   It was not a pleasant respite from her grief.   She actually wondered if we should even make this trip. Grandma and Grandpa Colombo also helped raise us while Mom and Dad worked. We loved being with them and we missed them both very much. Grandpa had told us he was a direct descendant of Christopher Columbus. That morsel of information was proudly passed down through the ages in his family who still reside in Genoa, Italy, where Cristoforo Colombo was born.

Nevertheless, we would continue with our plans. We drove to Alpena and arrived several hours after our breakfast with Dad.

Before heading to our cabin, Mom had to stop at a store for a few things.   She even bought us floaties. These elongated sponges assist in keeping someone afloat in water but were never meant to be a life-saving device. Regardless, Lily, Erik and I knew how to swim and Mom was an exceptionally strong swimmer. I hold no memory of these unfolding events just as the days prior to this day are forever erased.

Mom wanted us to help her unload the car and get things settled into the cabin. There's always a lot to do when a family is settling into a summer home bringing with them much needed supplies. The beautiful lake was beckoning. Mom had spent many happy summers enjoying that lake with her parents and her sisters. She knew the area well and knew where the drop-off bottom was. We so wanted to don our swimsuits and run into those crashing waves. Finally, Mom relented and told us we could go into the water but we had to stay close to the beach. Lily, Erik and I rode those waves with our floaties in hand. Erik wouldn't go any further than where his feet could touch bottom. It was hard to tell, however, where the bottom was; the sand beneath us was very uneven. The strong wind made the waves ferocious and we had drifted out in deep water, past the "drop-off point." Lily was fourteen years old. Did she know the danger lurking there? I was ten but I should have known too. I lost my floatie to the wind. I grabbed Lily's, causing her to lose her grip on it. Both floaties were gone.

I tried to grab onto Lily and was pulling her down. Lily tried to stand, but realized the water was way over her head. I was pushing her under the water and she had to pry me off in order to swim. She expected me to swim towards shore as she was. When she looked back, she saw me in the water; then I was gone. I didn't swim. I panicked. My brother Erik began to scream. The adults in the area saw me go under and tried to rescue me. The strong waves made it impossible. Had Lily not headed for the beach but stayed with me, we would have gone down together. There would have been two children, not just one, to save.

Back in Warren, Dad was meeting with some of his colleagues and Nana was in her basement beauty shop giving Poppy a haircut. Nana was a Licensed Cosmetologist even though she hated doing other people's hair and makeup. Go figure. I guess you'd have to know Nana. Busia was enjoying her television programs in her bedroom. Little did they know the events transpiring two hundred and fifty miles away. It was then that the phone call came.

Grandma & Grandpa Colombo

Mom called Nana and asked if she'd heard from Dad. Nana replied that she had not. Mom calmly told Nana there'd been an accident. Nana Jane asked what had happened, thinking maybe we had been involved in a traffic fender bender with our vehicle. Mom proceeded to tell Nana that while swimming, I had gone under and was sucked into the waves. As Nana screamed while asking if I had drowned, Poppy Ralph ran into the room. Mom, still calm, responded in the affirmative adding that it was an accident as Nana accusatorily demanded to know how this could have happened. Nana was hysterical, even as she heard Mom tell her the helicopter had arrived. That knowledge offered a glimmer of hope for my survival. As Poppy took the phone to talk with Mom, Nana ran upstairs wailing to her mother. Busia, Nana and Poppy began their vigil.

Dad was already on his way to Alpena. He was going to ask Poppy to drive him. Instead, Dad's employer, in his generosity, ordered the company plane to fly him there. Dad landed at the airport the very same time the *Survival Flight Helicopter* did. The pilot of the private plane transporting Dad looked at him and encouragingly said, "No one sends out helicopters for an already dead child."

He was wrong. I was dead. I know this exactly the same as I know I am alive today.

A lady came knocking at the cabin door and told Mom her kids were fighting and causing problems. Mom thought to herself that she can't leave us alone for five minutes anywhere without us causing some type of upheaval. Mom went to get her shoes, thinking not much else. It wasn't until she walked onto the beach that she saw an unsettling scene. No one knew anything for sure except that a child was under water, and the crashing waves rendered him unreachable. As people were running around on shore, Mom ran into the water shouting for someone to call 911. All she knew at that point was that someone was in trouble. She didn't know it was me until she saw only two of her three children in the water.

Mom still doesn't know how she managed, or how she did anything. She just remembers rushing into the trembling waves. Not knowing where to swim or how to find me, she followed the basic direction where several young men were diving under water looking for me. A couple of people swam past her on their way back to shore apologizing; for they were drowning themselves.

The wind was fierce. When Mom saw the two young men who had been searching for me heading towards the beach, she knew there was no one left to save me. The endeavor was hers alone. It was then that she felt the overwhelming power of her parents' presence guiding her to where I was.

She had grown up swimming in that lake and knew I had drifted beyond the drop off point. As she swam, she took deep breaths and dove into the deep; about twelve to fourteen feet. She saw me in a jack-knifed position at the bottom of the lake. She did what the others couldn't. She swam beneath me and shoved me to the surface with all of her might. She swam with me in tow towards a dock; then walked the rest of the way. Mom said I was so heavy it felt like she was carrying the weight of the world in her arms. There were many people waiting along the shore. They joined in the rescue and assisted Mom in lifting me onto the dock where she immediately began CPR. She said she knew things seemed bleak as I began to expel water and sand from my lungs. I was cold, blue and lifeless.

I saw myself lying on the dock with Mom feverishly trying to revive me. I saw the ambulance and all the people. From where I was, I could see everything, except I didn't know where I was. But, I wasn't alone. Grandma and Grandpa were with me. I didn't remember why or how, but I knew they had been with me within a great body of water.

The fire department arrived quickly and used their life-saving devices on me, frantically trying to revive me. The paramedics took over as they placed me into the ambulance which wasn't going anywhere. They would not let Mom enter. Mom knew there was little hope from the interminable amount of time that the ambulance remained stationary. It was determined that I would be taken to the hospital in Alpena. In the Emergency Room in Alpena, the attending physician did not seem optimistic. About an hour later, he came back to talk to Mom to give her some good news. He said, "I don't know how, but his kidneys are working; he's making urine." Mom knew dead people do not produce urine. I was. He explained that they had packed my body in ice to lower my temperature and that I would be flown to Ann Arbor with my body kept in a hypothermic state.

Dad was already re-united with Mom, Lily and Erik. They packed everything Mom had brought with her into Mom's car and journeyed to C. S. Mott Children's Hospital several hours away. Meanwhile, Poppy, Nana, Uncle Jonathan and Aunt Kelly were driving there from Warren. No one really knew the University of Michigan campus in Ann Arbor and Poppy had even been stopped by the police who then offered their assistance, pointing Poppy in the right direction.

Uncle Jonathan is Dad's youngest brother. Aunt Kelly is his wife. They have a boy, my cousin Andrew and a girl, my cousin Annaliese. My cousin Autumn would be born a few years later. Dad and Uncle Jonathan also had another brother, James. He was younger than Dad but much closer to him in age than Jonathan. He had married Aunt Lisa and they had two little girls, my cousins Asher and Brynn. All of us were still reeling from the death of Uncle James. He was diagnosed with brain cancer in February of 2004 and died on St. Patrick's Day. Uncle James' middle name was Patrick. I'll never forget it.

It was Saturday night. Nana, Poppy, Uncle Jonathan and Aunt Kelly arrived at U of M's Mott Children's Hospital, but not before Poppy called Father Bob, the Pastor of our church. St. Mark Roman Catholic Church in Warren was where we worshiped and had made very close friends with many of the parishioners. They were family to us. Poppy was retired but now helped out at St. Mark as the business manager. Even Grandma and Grandpa had attended Mass there. Father Bob immediately sent out e-mails asking as many people as he could to pray for me and for my family. The morning after my accident, he announced to all the congregation of the tragedy that had just occurred. He asked for more prayers.

Walking into the hospital, Nana, Poppy, Uncle Jonathan and Aunt Kelly were greeted by a huge painting. Nana immediately recognized it and saw it as a good omen.

An Extraordinary Sunday

When I was little, Nana used to encourage my interest in art. I especially liked to look at all her art books where she would show me the classics, the many techniques, the progression of art through the ages and the different styles of the artists. One painting in particular caught my eye and I have loved it ever since. It's called, Sunday Afternoon on the Island of La Grande Jatte by Georges-Pierre Seurat, or as Nana referred to it; "Sunday in the Park with George" from the Musical inspired by the painting where the chorus sings, "An Ordinary Sunday." It's a Neo-Impressionist painting done entirely by applying paint with thousands of dots instead of brush strokes. In my fascination, I would refer to it again and again.

I can remember visiting Dad's friend's family once where I saw a magnet on their refrigerator which was a miniature of this painting. None of the adults could understand my excitement over this particular magnet. I begged to borrow it so I could show it to Nana. Dad's friend was so amused he told me it was mine. I couldn't wait to bring the magnet to Nana. She still has it on her refrigerator to this very day.

Nana said she was determined to bring me into that great hall where my favorite painting was hanging in Mott Children's Hospital and show it to me herself. As she said this, everyone agreed, even though none of them knew if I was even alive. All they knew was that I was being helicoptered to U of M and that I had been under water for a very long time. Poppy had called Aunt Lisa and told her what had happened. All she would tell my cousins, Asher and Brynn, was that "Corey needed their prayers now more than ever."

It was a long time before any word came to my family about me, and all they were told was that since I drowned in freshwater and that the water was cold, it was an advantage. They weren't told that besides the original cardiac arrest I had had in the water, I had another in the hospital emergency room and yet another in the helicopter. Apparently, I had been resuscitated to a certain point and then lost once again. It's a mystery as to why anyone fought to save me anyway. My mother said everyone knew I was dead.

The Alpena Fire Department initially brought me to the hospital; and for many months after my accident, would call my mom to see how I was doing. They said I inspired them to never give up hope on accident victims.

643 & 36

When Uncle James was in high school, he had a part-time job at a local clothing store where he would help keep everything in order. He would tidy up the different departments, carry merchandise, wash windows and do other assigned tasks. Dad helped get him this job. Dad was a senior in high school by then and was a sales associate working in the men's department. Everyone who worked there knew Michael and James, the Lafferty brothers. Dad and Uncle James enjoyed their co-workers' company and everyone seemed to work well together. Ralph and Jane, their parents, would go to the store often. They would hear number 36 being paged over the loudspeaker and know their son "Jamey" was being summoned to destinations in his travels throughout the store. Nana and Poppy especially liked to come around and see what Dad and Uncle James were up to. It was during that time that Uncle James became associated with the number 36.

After Uncle James died, in her desperation to still have a connection to him, Nana began to see the number 36 appear at what she considered appropriate events in her life. Just as her father's 643 social security/lottery number would comfort her, Uncle James' store number, 36, began to make its appearance. Nana likened it to a wink from God; an assurance that Uncle James could still reach her.

During that interminably long night in the hospital waiting for word of my arrival and prognosis, Nana wept. Aunt Kelly reminded her that this was "Coriander" who was fighting for his life. Nana liked to call me "Coriander Spice Boy" and I found it to be quite endearing. My older brother Erik even had a little argument with Mom over it. He insisted that my middle name was "Ander." Mom told him it was Thomas. I was Corey Thomas Lafferty but Nana could call me anything she wanted.

Nana sat alone in the hall for some time. She didn't know how many times she had looked at the elevator across from her, but this time, there was something different. She noticed the number 36 posted next to it. She had been meditating and talking to Uncle James, telling him she knew he was aware of our family's sorrow and was doing his part; praying for me from the other side of life. It was odd that she had not noticed that number before but there it was; and to her, so was her son, Jamey. She did not know what to think however, and was very much afraid. When Uncle James was diagnosed with cancer, she felt her father's presence through the appearance of his number 643. Now she was seeing Jamey's number, 36. She realized 36 was intertwined with 643. It was different this time. Was this a little message from God that all would be well?

A God Wink

Mom and Dad arrived with my brother and sister in tow. They were drawn and worn. They were going through the necessary automated motions, as were my grandparents and my uncle and aunt. They were all numb and distraught.

As my life flashed before me, I was immersed in events with my family and friends. I suddenly woke up and felt like I was lying on a very soft and comfortable bed. The room was very bright although the light didn't hurt my eyes. I was somewhere very pleasant and saw my favorite toys. I was with Grandma and Grandpa who had recently died. Grandma had died three and a half months before my drowning and Grandpa, five and one half months before that. They both spoke to me and Grandpa asked me just what I thought I was doing. He said I shouldn't be there.

I was brought into my hospital room. My family stood around my bed. Dad cried and said my name. Mom cried with regret in her voice and said over and over again that she "knew better." There were no chairs around my bed and Mom simply sank to the floor while begging for me to come back. Mom needed her mother's comforting arms around her. Now there was only Michael's mother, her mother-in-law, who lost her own son and understood Mom's anguish. She went down to the floor to Mom, put her arms around her and gently raised her to the waiting chair that had been brought in. The attending nurses also brought cups of water for my family. My name was spelled out in big letters on the wall across from the foot of my bed. On the shelf was a little stuffed bear wearing a pin made of wings. The banner on the bear read, "I Rode the Survival Flight."

One of the nurses took my sister and brother to another room to make cards for me. My body temperature was kept down deliberately and I would remain comatose where I was attached to a variety of machines. There was nothing more to be done.

I was moving down a long hallway in this giant mansion that was very bright and full of white light. Grandma and Grandpa took me to

Uncle James who had died some three years before; and he took me to Dziadek, my great-grandfather. Uncle James said to tell the family he was fine and how much he loved us.

Grandpa had already said I didn't belong there, and now Uncle James was giving me a message to take back to my family. I knew they wanted my visit to this wondrous place to be just that; a visit!

There were other signs that I was healing while in a coma. My mom told me that God sent two physicians to help.

About three weeks before my accident, my mom had taken my siblings and me to Washington D.C. We had visited the Holocaust Museum where I was very intrigued with the children's exhibit called The Story of Daniel. I was obsessed with "Daniel" and even convinced my mom to buy me some books from the museum gift shop about him. In addition, I have always been fascinated by Asian culture and talked about moving to China. (This has since changed to Japan.) At age ten, I was beset with China and again had several books about the country and culture.

When I was first brought into the ICU at the hospital, my attending physician was a young and gentle man named Dr. Wong. He was Chinese. His "right hand man" was the resident, "Daniel." Daniel always wore a yarmulke. (For those of you who don't know, a yarmulke is a skullcap religious Jews wear, especially to synagogue.) Although I do not remember them, Mom told me she "knew" God had sent them to care for and help heal me. She saw this as a positive sign from God.

Prayer is a Place

Everyone my family knew was praying for me. People we didn't even know reached out to us. It was as though everything everyone did to help us was a prayer. We were immersed in prayer even if it was not formally said. It was expressed through action and deed. At our church, the congregation prayed and some people cried when Father Bob told them that I had drowned. They immediately set out to put together a large banner with their names on it to send to me. Those names represented their prayer. Everyone in the hospital was praying for us through their words and deeds. The Mott Children's Hospital in Ann Arbor was well equipped to care for not just the patients, but for their families as well. Even the card my brother Erik made for me was a prayer of some sort. It read, "We went to Alpena, then we went to Wal-Mart, and then you drowned." He included that he was sorry he was "such a jerk" and signed his name.

After four days, Mom began to communicate with everyone through the computers available to the families of patients. She put together the *CarePages* update where our family and friends were informed of my progress. The first entry stated that the medication which was paralyzing me was being discontinued and that my body temperature was warming. The ventilator was turned to its lowest setting. There would be tests, but not right away. Mom was the best person to receive information from the doctors and in turn send it to family and friends. The doctors spoke to Mom in medical terminology which she would translate to a level that everyone else could understand. She also knew how grave the situation was. I had suffered three cardiac arrests. My lungs were filled with water and sand from the bottom of the lake. Also, the official record was that I had been without oxygen, a heartbeat, and flat-lined for fifty-five minutes!

Dziadek was playing checkers! There he was, just like before. He was playing checkers and he was cheating as he played. Dziadek's daughter, Nana's sister, was with him. I had never met her. My great-aunt, Helen, had died before my parents were even married. She had been born with spina-bifida and was confined to a wheelchair all of her life. Although she was seated in a wheelchair she floated towards me, smiling. She gave me a hug. Poppy's parents gave me their love too. I knew they were my great-grandparents without ever having seen them before.

My great-grandparents, my grandparents, Great-Aunt Helen, and Uncle James all told me I had to go back and live my life; but that I had to live it differently. They all advised me to care more about my schoolwork and take my education very seriously. They wanted me to pay closer attention to learning; and play with my friends only during free time. They expressed their love for me and wanted only the best for my future. I understood everything.

CarePages

I had an MRI and chest X-Rays. The night nurse reported that I opened my eyes during the night a few times when she called my name. I also pulled at my restraints. It was six days since I had drowned and a lot happened on June 29, 2007. I woke and recognized both of my parents standing at my bed. I was very scared and I was crying. I mouthed that I wanted to go home and they tried to take me off the ventilator. I went into a panic because my throat was swelling and I could not breathe fully on my own. I was fighting and tried to bite one of the doctors. It took my parents and three other adults to keep me down. I was sedated again and kept on the ventilator, but at least my parents knew I had some ability to understand and communicate. I had pneumonia.

There was minimal damage to my brain. The neurologists had a review with the radiologists to clarify the damaged area to my brain. They said it was remarkable; that ultimately, they would have to wait and see what I did on my own. In her entry into the *CarePages* that night, my mother wrote the word, *miracle*.

I was still heavily sedated but I managed to edge my breathing tube out a bit and it had to be readjusted. The medications were being lowered as were the ventilator settings. I was soon taken off the ventilator and able to breathe on my own. The chest X-Ray came back revealing that I no longer had pneumonia and my lungs were clear. Mom wrote that she couldn't thank everyone enough for all the prayers.

There was a great big "Snoopy" card in my room from the parishioners at St. Mark Parish. I also saw balloons, toys and more cards. People were sending gifts as well as their prayers. Even though I did not remember drowning, Mom said I apologized to her for doing that "twisty" thing in the water but that Grandma and Grandpa Colombo were with me while I was under the water. Looking through the window in my room, I saw Nana and Poppy walking down the hallway. From that short distance, they heard me ask if they had brought Busia with them. Busia was not with them, but my sitter was. She was the only elderly lady I would see. The lady sat down in a rocking chair and had what I would call a "schoolteacher" look about her. She wore glasses and pulled her hair back to the top of her head in a bun. Everyone else stood around my bed, smiling,

27

talking to me. I don't know why, but I looked at my brother Erik and told him he was "stupid."

I was allowed to move out of the ICU into a "stepdown" unit in the hospital. I still needed to be monitored, so I wasn't yet in a regular hospital room. I was experiencing withdrawal from the medications I was on as my body warmed to normal temperature. Tremors were coursing through me. The doctors were trying to wean me slowly off the oxygen. All was not well. I had a CT scan and an EEG of my brain. I was no longer aware of my surroundings and no one knew if it was due to seizures, swelling in my brain, or the medications. Mom said I seemed to be in my own little world. The following day, the test results showed no swelling or neurological changes. The EEG came back fine. Before my parents arrived that day, they were told I fell while trying to get out of bed. The doctors and nurses examined me and told Mom and Dad that I was alright. They were also told I managed to pull out two IV's as well. I discovered I was unable to talk.

It was soon after this that the elderly lady in the rocking chair was still keeping vigil over me even though I was transferred to another room. She had a look of concern about her this time. Things were getting better for me though. That night, Mom wrote in her *CarePages* report that I was playing with the controls on my bed, moving my head and feet up and down.

It was time for Occupational Therapy. My rehabilitation had officially begun. The therapist came to my room and had me pick out colors and draw a circle. I tried to draw a cartoon character, but got too tired. Before my accident, I was always drawing cartoon characters and I was very good at it too, even if I was only ten years old. The rehabilitation would continue at my bed until I was in a regular room, then I would actually go to the Rehabilitation Center in the hospital. It was decided that I would begin wearing my own clothes to give me a better sense of myself and my new surroundings. I had to have an X-Ray procedure called a Swallow Study as well in order to determine whether or not I'd be able to start eating and drinking liquids. They were concerned about my lungs.

Mom was asking for prayers for Dad. He was very emotional and having a difficult time as the visible signs of my disabilities were becoming obvious. Some of my brain cells were now dying and everyone wondered just how severe the brain damage would be. I would be having speech, occupational and physical therapy five days a week. The neurologist ordered another MRI. He explained that although the first MRI showed very little damage, the hypothermic treatment may have masked additional damage from showing in the first MRI. In other words, when my body temperature was raised back to normal levels, my brain cells that had been damaged finished dying. I was unable to safely drink liquids but I did have a few bites of scrambled eggs and about half a pancake. I also chose a movie to watch that evening.

On the sixth of July, Mom was telling everyone how I could not be still. Everyone tells me how I was in constant motion, moving every limb, sliding up and down and from side to side. I was extremely restless though it was involuntary. I was placed in a wheelchair and able to tolerate it for ten to fifteen minutes. I continued to be very active at all times as a result of the lowering of my medications. Mom was asking for continued prayers.

Finally, the MRI results were in. The neurologist reviewed them with my parents just as Nana and Poppy were walking into my room. I had some injury to the part of my brain which coordinates motor skills and speech. It was impossible to tell if or how much I would get back. There was a chance I would be mute. Up until then, I was a very loud, talkative child. The neurologist explained what he believed happened with my abilities deteriorating. Brain cells sometimes die a while after an injury. They were probably working fine at first then died a few days later when coming out of the hypothermic state. Mom expected this report and said with intensive therapy and more prayers, that anything was possible.

Rhyme and Reason

I was now in a private room. It was nice because I was able to have many visitors. My aunts and uncles and first cousins came to see me and I got to go outside for the first time. I rode in a wheelchair in the fresh air and sunshine. Mom said I smiled the whole time. My legs were very strong although I still didn't have my center of gravity. Mom uploaded pictures to everyone online. Back in my room, I had little control over my arms and hands as I tried to do some drawing. Mom said with determination, I would improve. I think my sitter in the rocking chair agreed as she smiled fondly.

A poster board with an alphabet was made up for me. Since I was unable to communicate orally, I would have to spell out words by pointing to the letters. There were also basic words I could point to. I enjoyed words, particularly words that rhymed. I loved stories and I especially loved poetry. From as far back as I can remember, Nana would read poems and Mom loved to read Dr. Seuss and Shel Silverstein to me. As I got older, I would read poems myself. I even began to write my own. Nana had a friend,

Justine Peña, who was a poet. She published a lot of her work and Nana was especially proud to know an author who gave her signed copies of her books. We enjoyed reading Mrs. Peña's poems together. When I donated my very long hair to *Locks of Love*, a cancer foundation, she wrote a poem especially about me. I was so thrilled and felt so honored. Something about me was actually in someone's book!

Corey

Sensitive, warm eyes
Beautiful flowing chestnut brown hair
Cascading to your shoulders,
You shook my hand
I yours
We met, reader and poet
And then
I learned
That beautiful, chestnut brown hair
Cascading around your shoulders
Would soon be cut short
Given with love
To children less fortunate, suffering
In need of feeling
Special, loved, pretty.
Your concern
Your sensitivity toward others

Is an example
Worthy of our notice
Worthy of our imitation.

Justine E. Peña
More Thoughts
© 2007

　　Mom and Dad, Lily and Erik officially checked out of the hospital's hotel that was available for patients' families. They would now be making the drive from Warren to Ann Arbor every day, as were Nana and Poppy and other relatives and friends. I was still trying to coordinate my arms and my fingers so I could point to the letters on my poster board. Great-Aunt Ann, Grandpa Colombo's sister, brought me a potholder craft kit. She and I had made potholders together before my accident. I mentally connected the making of potholders with the little loops on the frame to mentally connecting letters to make words, and words to form thoughts. I probably made the same connection to my drawings. I thought of myself as an artist from as long as I can remember.

Sunday in the Park

Mom and Dad were still taking me outside in the wheelchair. The July weather was extremely hot and we went through a sprinkler in the garden to cool off. I was not permitted to stand up on my own and I had no control over my arms.

We also went to visit another patient in the hospital who is a friend of our family. She was a little girl in her teens, battling cancer. Her family was surprised to see Nana and Poppy in the elevator as they didn't know what had happened to me. Nana and Poppy knew about Ashley, but they didn't know she was in Mott Children's Hospital. It was a bit of a relief seeing someone else that I knew as a patient there. She was in our prayers.

The hospital offered a lot of activities to do to keep me busy. I even got a chance to go to a concert in the hospital's community room given by a violinist and an acoustic guitarist. I love the violin and I enjoyed the concert a lot. One day soon I will buy a violin and take lessons! There were many events in the community room for patients and their families from pizza parties to magic shows. Celebrities would come to meet with us as well. We received gifts from the community. In addition to a game room with many computerized games, there was also a large outdoor screened-in playground with padded floors, a library, indoor play areas and well-stocked patient kitchens for nourishment. We truly felt special and well cared for. I particularly enjoyed seeing the artwork on the walls. Many hands went into helping us throughout our hospital stay.

Mom said I was cranky and agitated with my brother and sister, just like normal. The doctors said I would probably have to be in the hospital at least another three weeks. My rehabilitation was now taking place in the physical medicine area, which gave me a change of scenery. Mom and Dad had to take me there themselves. Mom bought me new "Spiderman" shoes for the occasion. A hospital psychologist assessed my cognitive abilities and said that I was at a ten year old level – meaning my comprehension was appropriate. I was given a new room, just outside the nurse's station. They wanted to keep an eye on me in case I tried to get out of bed during the night. I guess that's why the lady in the rocking chair followed me.

Nana was very interested in what I had to say as I pointed to the letters on the poster-board. She asked if I knew why I was in the hospital. Looking back all these years later, I have very vague and fuzzy memories of that time. I remember dreams that were crazy. They consisted of action figures and "Elmo" from *Sesame Street*, the children's program I watched years before. The dreams were nonsensical. I can identify them in typical, common terms. There was no substance to them. They were what everyone experiences and identifies with. They must have happened during my withdrawal period from the medication or maybe even during restless nights. My family tells me of what transpired and tells the stories over and over. I lost those months of my life in the hospital. What I clearly retained was the memory of my visit in Heaven; and that was what I wanted to tell Nana as I spelled out the amazing events which took place after I drowned.

The first sentence I spelled out was when I asked Nana if she knew that God was a girl. Nana replied that she did know and that her name is "Sophia." Sophia is the Greek word for wisdom. At ten years old, I didn't know anything about that. My family had already learned that I had been with Grandma and Grandpa Colombo, but I believe this was the first time I told them I was also with God.

It was with great difficulty that I was able to control my arms and fingers, but I had little trouble pointing to the letters. Everyone said I spelled out words so quickly they had trouble keeping up with me. Before my brain cells died, I was able to speak. Now, I could barely grunt nor could I control my lips or my tongue. My body was still in a constant state of movement and unrest. I kept pointing to the letters on the poster-board. I pointed to Poppy and spelled out the word, parents. I was communicating with him that I visited with his parents whom I had never met. Nana asked if I'd seen her sister. I shook my head no, that I didn't. She said she was disappointed that Aunt Helen couldn't be bothered to take the time to see me. I can only explain this discrepancy as a result of my excitement and frustration. I most certainly was with Aunt Helen, or Cioci, as Dad called her. I never saw her before either, yet I knew who she was and what her relationship was to me.

Nana asked if I had seen Jesus. I shook my head that yes, I had! I began to spell out "He gave me…." when Erik excitedly interrupted and shouted, "Life!" I vigorously shook my head in the affirmative. We all smiled.

The flight nurse from the Survival Flight Helicopter which transported me to Ann Arbor from

Alpena the night I drowned came to see me. Mom and Dad stood around my bed along with Nana and Poppy. They all heard him say that in his seventeen years of experience, he could only report of one other drowning victim surviving. He told us he knew there was no hope for me as I had a cardiac arrest as the helicopter was landing. That was why it took such a terribly long time before my family was able to see me. He was as confounded by my recovery as everyone else. He also said I'd be able to tour the helicopter when I was ready. The helicopter was parked just outside the main doors of the hospital and my family and friends saw it whenever they visited. A few weeks later, I did see the inside of the helicopter that flew me to the hospital identifying it with a big "M"; the shortened version for the University of Michigan.

The neurologist told Mom and Dad the doctors were considering the possibility of having me on medication which they use for Parkinson's patients. It might help with the lack of control of my arms and tongue. They thought they would wait to see what effect my rehabilitation had on my limbs. I enjoyed therapy. I made a dot painting (was "Sunday in the Park" an inspiration?) and I even bowled a little. I also was on the computer as part of my therapy. My balance was getting better and I was very eager to run. Mom and Dad took me to dinner in the cafeteria. I could not make my arms reach my mouth, so I needed help to eat. Mom kept up with her reports to everyone in the *CarePages* entries. Friends and families of friends and their families were now following my progress.

July Melts into August

The hospital had a Harry Potter Party and I spent a couple of hours learning how to use a magic wand and make potions. I made a clay snake and played some games. I even won a copy of the new book coming out about Harry Potter. I had a great time. I was doing better with balance and I tried to run and climb. I didn't want to stay in bed anymore. The rehabilitation therapists insisted I stay in bed and I could see, by the look of the lady who was watching me from her rocking chair, that I should probably comply. I had a feeding tube in me even though I was allowed to eat some soft foods during the day. The tube feedings were increased during the night and made me so sick I vomited. Afterwards, I was pale and sad. I was very down-hearted about my situation; not being able to use my hands or communicate. Mom said she was frustrated too and that we had to stay positive. As she was leaving that evening, I cried. Mom asked everyone to keep praying for me that I may be granted strength.

My brother Erik spent time with me in the activity room playing on a Nintendo Wii. I was upset that I couldn't maneuver the controls very well but Mom and Dad said I was doing great and my skills would come back in time. Actually, I did better on the game than Mom did. My speech would seem to come and go in speech therapy, so that was encouraging. I was beginning to miss the things I used to be able to do and took for granted. I even began to feel angry. Mom was a little angry too.

In one of the response entries to the *CarePages* book, the lady who knocked at our cabin door, who told Mom her "kids were fighting," said her nephew and his friend were the ones who saved me as she admittedly stated they could not swim. She also wrote that it was she who gave me CPR. Everyone who was there knew this was not true. Non-swimmers could not save a drowned person from the bottom of a lake. The water was very deep and no one even knew where I was. Mom responded kindly and thanked these people for their assistance. The police report did not validate or agree with this lady's account.

I was prescribed Parkinson's medication and it was hoped it would help me to form words. On the contrary, Mom thought it would only make it harder. The physicians said they would make some adjustments to the dosage. Erik actually helped feed me. I would only eat the cheese from the ravioli he gave me but I did eat the strawberry applesauce, hash browns and the lemon ice. It was hoped the feeding tube would be removed soon. I could not feel the pressure in my mouth so I didn't know how hard to chew and how to push food to the back of my throat with my tongue. Another Swallow Study would be performed to determine if it was safe for me to eat any types of food or drink anything at all. It wasn't.

Mom and Dad were informed that upon my discharge, the therapists wanted me close to my parents at home, especially during the night. Also, since I was always a very hyper child, they wanted me to stay calm and not become too excited about anything. People with brain injuries tend to be very excitable. I listened to music with Dad and we played checkers. I watched a lot of television, especially Nickelodeon, as well as the Disney Channel. Mom took me shopping in the hospital gift shop. That was fun. I pointed out many of the things I wanted. In the following days, I took Mom and Dad on a tour of the hospital. I actually took them to the cafeteria, the gift shop, the hospital's hotel and the rehabilitation center. Mom said I did this a lot better than many people who follow the signs and still get lost. I didn't lose my way at all. We even went through some stormy weather together. There was a tornado warning and we all had to take cover. There was another day where I won a treasure hunt and was able to choose my prize - a bubble gun. It's the same as a water gun; just shoots bubbles. I played air hockey and many other games. Mom said I was so good at the games the other children might not want to play with me anymore. I did a lot of exercising in therapy and everyone was tired out just watching me. I liked to relax afterwards in my room reading the books people were kind enough to send me. Nana said her greatest joy was simply watching me smile while I was lying in bed, enjoying the cartoons on television. She said it was then she would give thanks and realize how blessed we were. Everyone said my recovery was remarkable. That word was not totally correct. My recovery was: *a miracle.*

My sister Lily was exhibiting deep emotional problems. She was not sleeping well or feeling well. Mom said her role in all the events which led to my drowning was causing her distress. Looking back at it now, I can only wonder what she must have been thinking and feeling. Mom requested prayers for her as well as for me. Nana and Poppy remembered how Erik tried to comfort me when I was agitated. He held down my arms and kissed my forehead. They appreciated Lily's efforts; reading to me and playing games with me. Nana and Poppy tried to soothe my brother and sister by taking them to their house for a meal, then spending the evening in Uncle Jonathan and Aunt Kelly's backyard pool where they played with our little cousin Andrew. The adults, including Busia, my great-grandmother, would enjoy the evening sitting on the deck watching them. My aunts, Mary, Sue and Karen, also helped out with my brother and sister, inviting them to spend time with them and my uncles and cousins.

One night, Lily and Mom stayed the night at the hospital with me. Lily climbed in bed with me and we watched a scary movie together. (I love scary movies, so it was good.) My roommate at the time was in a lot of pain and she screamed all night long. The three of us felt very sorry for her. We never got any sleep that night, but I still enjoyed having my mom and sister with me.

I was progressing well. My parents would do my therapy with me when I didn't have an actual therapist. I had a very difficult time bringing my jaw up to close my mouth. When I did, I couldn't keep it closed for long. I was, however, doing very well on the computer keyboard using the mouse in order to visit websites. But I still couldn't feed myself or keep a bowl in front of me without knocking it away while trying to maneuver a spoon into it.

You Only Live Twice

The Principal from my school came to see me. I was surprised and excited. She brought Floam, the gooey-spongy stuff that has little Styrofoam balls mixed with goo. Even my parents played with it. It proved to be a stress-reliever as I was becoming angry. Later, I resorted to drawing whenever I was angry or upset. This always relaxes me and makes me feel happy. Mom said I was beginning to recognize that something had happened to me and all that it wrought. I was even showing my temper to my therapists. Even eating was too much of a chore because of the lack of control I had with my mouth and arms. Later, I would be happy; blasting my iPod, jumping up and down on my bed, pretending to sing with the music. Mom would make me stop because she was afraid I'd fall and get hurt.

The therapists said my left arm was improving and they were going to teach me to be left handed. They said they would work with both my arms, encouraging my drawing skills. My Parkinson's medication was increased. If that didn't improve my ability to move my mouth, it would be eliminated altogether. A different medication was considered which helps the brain multi-task. One part of my brain needed more dopamine and the other needed less. It was difficult to find a balance.

My third grade teacher came to see me and brought her children. I enjoyed their visit but later became very sick. I had been having migraines since I was very little and they continued even after my accident. I was also very nauseated. This was normal for me. After waking from a deep sleep, I was fine. I was always delighted to be able to run around with my brother and sister, my cousins and my friends. Many people from my elementary school, Green Acres in Warren, posted a lot of response entries into the *CarePages* notes Mom was writing.

My parents were getting their room at home ready in order to be able to accommodate a bed in it for me. I had officially kicked my "drug addiction" and was no longer on valium or methadone. I liked the nurses who were taking care of me and I liked my roommate, Ryan. I also liked the lady sitting in the rocking chair, always watching me. I wanted to work harder in therapy because I wanted to go home. The doctors explained to me that I would be getting a stomach tube and that scared me. Dad was with me as the nurse showed me what it actually looked like.

My first and second grade teachers came to see me. They brought me gifts. I was excited about their visit. I was also excited about the bowling fundraiser being planned for me by some of the people at the hospital my mom worked at but I wouldn't be released from the hospital in time. I wanted to be there to sign autographs. I was very emotional and angry about this.

My mood swings were not uncommon. Dad tried to explain the brain injury and how it affected my inability to do the simple things that I never gave any thought to before. I couldn't understand what had happened. I thought I had hit my head somewhere. I had no memory of any trauma of any kind.

Look Homeward Angel

The only thing that was clear to me was my incredible visit in Heaven. It was at the highest level of consciousness that I had ever been. I saw images of my life, playing with my favorite toys with my friends, Natalie and Alex. It was love, happiness and joy. It was an unearthly, mystical realm which went on forever where everything seemed to be happening at once. I understood all it expressed. All the people I saw, my deceased family members, seemed to appear and disappear all at the same time. We were in a never-ending mansion full of light and peace. It was a place of pure love. My family there loved me so very much and I loved them.

One day, Mom wrote in her CarePages entry that I tried to "break out" of the hospital. It seemed I thought I'd greet my parents on my own at the hospital's entrance door. I made it all the way to the second floor before security caught up with me. Multiple people were searching for me. Since my attempted "escape," I was tethered; literally. They placed a protection alarm system around my ankle so I couldn't leave my sixth floor room without setting off the alarm. The only time the tether came off was when my parents were with me.

I was looking forward to my day with Dad when the hospital staff would take us on an outing to see how well I would do in public. I was asked if I wanted to go to Domino Farms or the Shopping Mall. I asked if there was a bookstore in the Mall. Since there was, the choice was easy. Dad and I were taken to the Mall.

In therapy, I made a HOPE bead necklace. Each bead represented an accomplishment, therapy, or procedure I had gone through. Dad still has this necklace. Everyone in the family tried to remain optimistic. The speech therapist told Mom and Dad he didn't think I'd ever be able to eat normally again or speak clearly again. This made my dad very angry. Mom said I surprised everyone in all other aspects of my recovery and didn't see why I wouldn't continue to do so. That night she requested more prayers for me as she wrote her CarePages post. Dad was still very depressed and sad.

Before I could be released from the hospital, I had to have a feeding tube put into my stomach. So the doctors surgically inserted my feeding tube. I came through the procedure very well. I was in a lot of pain but that was normal. My parents would use the tube to insure my nutrition at home. I also discovered that after being released from the hospital, I would be going to therapy not far from our home. Arrangements were being made for the continuation of my schoolwork. Unfortunately, I was unable to attend the upcoming Bowling Fundraiser, but I was there in spirit. I made it clear to Mom that I would rather have the nasal tube than the stomach tube. She told me I would feel differently in a few days after the pain subsided. I was irritable because I was very thirsty and unable to drink any water. That would continue until I could swallow well. Mom told me I couldn't drink anything when we got home. That did not go over well with me, but my sitter, the lady in the rocking chair, gave me an encouraging smile.

A nurse entered my room one morning and introduced herself. She asked my parents if I had told them about all the excitement I had caused the night before. They looked at me and recognized my familiar mischievous look. I think for a moment they enjoyed the "reunion." They replied they knew nothing. The nurse proceeded to tell them that after they had left the previous night, I was told I was to wear a tether again.   Since I hadn't worn a tether in a few days I was very upset and threw a temper tantrum. The nurse placed it on my ankle anyway, after which I kicked my tray table out into the hall, yelling and screaming as hard as I could.   Since everyone was ignoring me, I then began to roll my cans of liquid nutrition out of my room, sending them through the hallway. I had twenty-four cans to work with. The nursing staff finally had enough and called security. A giant security guard peered into my room, caught me in the act, and wondered out loud if there was a "problem." I stood up, looked at him, backed up, and quickly jumped into my bed. The nurses never heard another sound from me the rest of the night, nor did I ever complain about the tether again.

The lady in the rocking chair seemed quite amused and content as her eyes beamed at me, lovingly.

In her daily report to everyone, Mom said she hoped in the future I would publish all my experiences during this hospital stay.

Heaven Can Wait

It was August, 2007. Nana's prediction proved true. I gazed at Georges Seurat's beautiful *Sunday Afternoon on the Island of La Grande Jatte* painting in the hallway at Mott Children's Hospital, University of Michigan in Ann Arbor.

I had survived! I drowned, I died, I went to Heaven and I came back!

I was leaving the hospital never to be the same as I was before that fateful day. I was unable to talk or use my hands, but I could point to the alphabet poster board and spell out words faster than anyone could keep up.

After I was discharged and before we went home, we stopped at Nana and Poppy's house to see Busia, my great-grandmother. She had not seen me since the day before I drowned. Erik and I ran up the stairs to her room where she was sitting in her rocking chair. She beamed with joy as she extended her arms to us both. We hugged and hugged. Even though Busia was in her early 90's, she had no trouble going up and down the stairs. She came down with us to the family room where she joined Mom, Dad, Lily, and Nana and Poppy. She wanted to know everything I could tell her through my alphabet poster board. She was thrilled to hear that I saw my great-grandfather, Dziadek, in Heaven and that he was still cheating at playing checkers. I asked Busia if she knew that God is a girl.

Even though Grandma and Grandpa Colombo were talking to me, as was Uncle James, there was no confusion as I found myself in the presence of Jesus. Every sense of dialogue and communication was crystal clear. I understood the connection we all have to one another and how we are all one in the universe.

Grandma and Grandpa Colombo were telling me how important my education was and what I had to do. It was incumbent upon me to be kind and understanding to others and know what truly mattered in life. I had to continue to grow in many ways. I had to accomplish my dreams and create my happiness on Earth.

I felt tremendous love for all the people who were there and the immeasurable love they had for me. I wanted so to remain with them. Grandpa said, "Heaven would wait." Uncle James was telling me that I could not stay. He added that he did not want to leave Aunt Lisa and my cousins Asher and Brynn, but didn't have a choice.

My thoughts then turned to our family on Earth.

Jesus asked me what I wanted to do. I knew He was Jesus. I just knew I was in His presence. He wore a dazzling white robe. He was the very essence of care, compassion, empathy and understanding. His love extended beyond measure not just to me but to everyone. He said I should go back to the living and live my life.

At the same time, God bent down towards me as She swept me up unto Herself. She embraced me as a loving mother hugs her child.

She delighted in me. There was no time or separation between us. She explained to me that my family was crying for me and that the people in church were praying for me. I felt the love radiating from her. With Her, I was safe and secure.

I then told God I missed my family.

Jesus reached out to me and smiled.

Suddenly, I saw Dad flying in an airplane as I was transported through a large doorway above which was the letter **M**.

Uncle Jonathan and Aunt Kelly came over to Nana and Poppy's house with Andrew and Annaliese to celebrate my homecoming. Uncle Jonathan got down on his knees, wrapped me in his arms, and sobbed. Someone said I had a guardian angel watching over me. Nana said she didn't believe in angels. I stepped back from Jonathan's embrace. Amazed at what she had just said, I spelled out to Nana from my poster-board that while in the water, angels were all around me. Since to this very day I don't remember drowning, I can't explain how I know that. This statement, along with not remembering seeing her sister in Heaven, caused Nana's skepticism towards my story to grow. I told everyone the angels were in every drop of water! How does anyone separate individual drops of water from the body of water itself? And Grandma and Grandpa Colombo were there too!

When we got home, there was a large banner greeting me which had been made and signed by the people from our church. I was excited to see it. It read, "Welcome Home Corey!" and was decorated with pictures of Transformers and Spiderman. There were also more cards and some little presents from my family. I was settled at home now and my bed was in Mom and Dad's room. Mom said it was odd that mixing my medications made her nervous when all these years she always felt confident when mixing medication for her patients. We had dinner together and then went for a walk. I even played with one of the neighborhood children for a little while until a football hit me in the stomach. We then went to a department store where I bought some drumsticks that connect to my iPod which allows me to play drums. They are much quieter than real drums so it was fine with Mom and Dad. (Later on, I really did acquire a real set of drums and played cymbals and bass drums in the school band.)

That night, Mom wanted me settled in bed so she could connect my feeding tube. It had to run for eight hours but she knew the bag would be empty after six hours, so to her, it was like having a baby again; regular formula and scheduled feedings. Everyone was trained to administer my feeding tubes, even Nana and Poppy.

I was looking forward to attending my therapy sessions and meeting new people. Mom and Dad were disappointed and concerned that my therapy was not exactly what U of M had coordinated for me. Also, Mom was not convinced the medications I was on were of much benefit. She moved heaven and earth to get me to the right physicians and the right therapy. Mom was still posting in my *CarePages* book and told everyone that I looked forward to visits and outings but felt a little downhearted. She requested prayers for me as my sister and brother and all my friends were going back to school and I wasn't. I was only ten years old and having some very tough days, as everyone expected. I would get angry and frustrated and fight with everyone in the family. I wanted everything to be the way it was before my accident. Mom tried to find a therapist I could talk to which wasn't easy because of the communication barrier. Eventually, I ended up with my brother Erik's psychologist, Dr. William Irving, who I still see today. Overall, I had more good moments than bad, but Mom wanted to get me the help I needed. I hated my feeding tube and pulled on it when I was upset. I would sneak things I couldn't have and eat and drink when I thought it was safe and no one was looking.

Mom took me to the doctor suspecting that I was developing pneumonia. She was concerned about my lungs. She was still straightening things out with the insurance company for my rehabilitation program. Mom wanted different doctors. She honored all my U of M follow-up appointments. The cost for my medical care was about $10,000 a month and Mom and Dad had to find other resources to help pay for it. My parents had so very much to do. Mom liked a pediatric neurologist at St. John Hospital where she worked. She made an appointment with him. He spent almost an hour with us. Mom said he gave me the most thorough examination/evaluation that anyone had done. He concluded that I would be recovering for probably the next two to three years and to never give up hope. It was decided that I would slowly come off the Parkinson's medication and another medication would be tried once the dopamine was discontinued. Mom did not like to medicate, ever, unless it was really necessary.

Although my progress has slowed down due to my age now, the doctors still see progress in my strength, control and motor skills I currently only take two different medications; one which helps control muscle tremors and spasms in my arms, and the other helps decrease the amount of saliva I make, which helps me speak more clearly.

Come September

Mom and the school district coordinated my continuing education. They didn't want to do too much after a brain injury for at least three months. There was still a lot of healing for the brain to do on its own. Different parts of my brain were now working to send signals to the rest of my body and it was necessary not to "short circuit" those commands and efforts. Mom's girlfriend, Marylee, brought over a three wheel trike bike which was considered safe for me to ride and helped to build up muscle. (I have since progressed to my regular two wheel bike, which I ride on occasion. I have recently finished driver's education and have my driving permit.)

The doctor who took care of me in the emergency room in Alpena right after I drowned submitted an entry into my *CarePages*. He wrote, "Hi Corey, this is Dr. Chapman. We were just thinking about you way up here in Alpena. I know you do not know me. I took care of you when you were here. I asked if anyone had heard how you were doing and we found your website. I'm really pleased that you are doing so well. Keep up your good spirits and I wish you the best. I think someone upstairs has something important for you to do with your life. Best regards, D. Chapman, M.D."

We went to St. Mark, our church in Warren, for the first time since my accident. I enjoyed seeing everyone. Our pastor, Father Bob, called me up to the altar so the congregation could see a living miracle. Father Bob had no doubt that I experienced the supernatural after I drowned. He had been a hospital chaplain. He had heard after-death accounts similar to mine from patients to whom he ministered.

A few days after I had come out of my coma, Nana told Mom that Father Bob said Mom had given me life twice. The first time was when I was born; the second when she rescued me from the bottom of the lake. Mom became emotional and didn't want to hear it. The memory of the trauma was still too raw. She didn't want to relive her role in it. Dad also was emotional. He thought had he been with us on the trip to Alpena, we would not have gone further into the water than we should have. We might have stayed close to the shore as we were told. As was normal, there were feelings of regret and guilt. We all had them. They would continue to plague us every now and then and in the coming years. The important thing was to not dwell on the past but look forward to a positive future.

I would be immersed in therapy and treatment. Also, a teacher would be coming to our house for my school instruction. Lily was in band and choir at school and Erik was in football. Mom and Dad had some weddings to attend and they even managed to take us to a couple of church festivals. They even let me go on some of the rides. I was happy to see some of my friends there. I also got to attend my school's open house where I saw many friends and all three of my fifth grade teachers, the media specialist and the music teacher. My school held a Spaghetti Dinner Fundraiser for me and many people attended. The organizers even bought little gifts for my sister Lily and my brother Erik. It was heartwarming to see all the people who came and who cared. Some of them were people who only knew me through their relatives and friends. At the end of the evening, I stood at the microphone and managed to inflect what I hoped sounded like a heartfelt "thank you." It was the best I could do.

I was going to rehabilitation at the Detroit Medical Center (DMC) Brain Injury Center five days a week. I was doing very well. Dad was taking me.

Mom was back at work and Dad had taken a leave of absence. I was beginning to speak a little and move my tongue a little more. I was also able to keep my mouth closed for a little longer length of time. I was eating with great difficulty but I was enjoying it a little more. Mom and Dad were hoping I would soon be able to have thickened liquids. I was beginning to hate all the appointments I had to go to but it was just the way things had to be. My hands had not improved much and I was given a brace to wear on my right hand to keep the wrist straight. I was on a waiting list for using a machine that would stimulate the nerves in my mouth. Eventually I received "vitastim" therapy on my mouth and neck muscles. This has significantly helped me regain more use of my tongue and mouth for speaking and eating.

This reminds me that I want to extend a special and heartfelt "thank you" to my occupational therapist, Beth Angst, who took great delight in "electrocuting me" during my sessions.

I was off all of my medications but still on the feeding tube. I was being fed five times a day instead of all night long. Mom said it was the same as when your baby finally starts to sleep all through the night.

Mom had purchased all of my medical records. She entered some of the information into the *CarePages* that she was still posting for relatives and friends. After reading the dire reports, she wrote that we were truly blessed.

I was without oxygen and a heartbeat for fifty-five minutes! My recovery was explained in unconvincing terms. The medical terminology was a practical and mostly failed attempt at describing what really happened.

What really happened was: *a miracle*!

The Heaven Connection

As Christmas was drawing near, holiday decorations were everywhere. The waiting room in the rehabilitation center where I went for therapy was no exception. Near the entrance was a large decorated tree which would have been the most prominent symbol in that room, except for the very large figure standing alone at its side. Nana pointed to it and made mention that it was an angel. I shook my head and tried to tell her that it didn't look anything like an angel. She understood what I was trying to say. She asked me then what I thought angels should look like? I couldn't tell her. But I did tell her they looked nothing like that statue. I do remember the angels. They did not have wings. They looked like people. I knew they were angels and they were all around me in the water; they were in every drop.

Nana did not believe my after-death experience was of any supernatural origin. She was convinced that a part of my brain protected me from the trauma I endured; consoling me with extraordinary pictures. Everything I had relayed was what I already knew. I saw my life pass before me with familiar friends and my favorite toys. I knew Grandma and Grandpa, my great-grandfather Dziadek and my uncle, James. It also stood to reason that I would recognize Jesus because of my religious education from my parents, catechism at church, and everything Nana herself had told me.

Nana had suggested that the Supreme Being would be of a female nature as well and not just a kindly grandfatherly figure with a long beard and white hair. Whenever we would talk of Heaven, she would ask me if I thought perhaps I was relaying a pre-conceived notion. She said it was probably a spectacular occurrence of the mind since we knew so little about our brains and never used them to their full capacity anyway. Dad and Poppy would tell her to let me have these pleasant memories and leave them at the level I thought they were. But throughout the years, she would persist. She was skeptical. I think what she didn't realize was that it made sense that God would provide my visit in Heaven with what I could comprehend. That's why Dziadek was playing checkers and my great-aunt Helen, or "Cioci," was in a wheelchair. Cioci certainly didn't need a wheelchair in Heaven anymore than Dziadek would be playing checkers.

I was unable to communicate anything after I drowned. I couldn't talk. Even if I could have found the words to describe what I knew to be true, I wouldn't have been able to define Heaven in any earthly terms anyway; adding to that my very limited vocabulary concerning the mystical. However, I did have the comprehension level of any child almost eleven years old. I was able to discern the difference between fantasy and reality.

Mom had no reservations about my heavenly experience. She knew it was true. She had felt the power of her parents' presence during my rescue. They were guiding her. I can't imagine what it was like for her. She swam into the lake looking for me. Other people were trying to find me under the water but were unable to. She couldn't see anything but she kept on swimming out into the deep. The waves were very strong. She found me floating under the water above the sand in a jack-knifed position. She said what astounded her most was when I came out of my coma and could still talk (before my brain cells died) I described my position at the bottom of the lake. She said I could not have known that, as she never told anyone about it. I also said I saw Dad flying in an airplane. I added that I saw the outside of the hospital with the large "M" for Michigan. I could not have known that either.

I knew of the danger the lake held. Mom told me to stay near the shore in the shallow water. Busia had warned me the night before to be careful. She remembered Dziadek always telling everyone to respect the power of the water. That is true of any natural force. Poppy told me to be careful in the water. There were many warnings to me from the adults in my family. The subsequent events unfolded into a preventable tragedy but then took on a supernatural nature. Grandma and Grandpa intervened from Heaven. Everyone seemed to be looking out for me.

Mom and Dad wanted to celebrate my recovery by thanking everyone for their prayers and support with a big party. My 11th birthday was drawing near and fell in line at just the right time. A thanksgiving celebration and the anniversary of my birth coincided to provide all the more reason to invite everyone we knew. I was alive and flourishing on December 20, 2007, after drowning on the previous June 23rd. The party was going to be held in December in the St. Mark Parish Gathering Space and I was looking forward to seeing all the people I already knew were coming. The event was catered with a lot of food and many activities for all the children. Mom even brought in a karaoke machine for people to sing along with. We had a grand time. I stood with my family as Deacon George prayed over us and all the guests. We were celebrating our connection to God and one another whether we thought of it or not; whether we knew it or not. It was a profound moment for me.

In the *CarePages* entry, Mom thanked everyone for coming to the party and wished them much happiness and good health in the coming New Year. She told everyone that I would be going to school for a half day only in the morning starting January 7, 2008. My therapy would take place in the afternoon. I had to wear a brace/splint on my right arm and I hated it. But I was excited to be back in school. I was so fortunate because I was right where I should have been, scholastically. I was glad to see my friends again. They all knew what had happened to me and they knew I was different. I now had disabilities. Our planned trip to Disneyworld had to be cancelled and this actually brought Aunt Mary to tears. She was so looking forward to her entire family being together there after all everyone had been through. We eventually did go to Disneyworld, but we had to wait until my brain had healed more. Since then, we've been back for several visits!

I had speech therapy five days a week, physical therapy two to three days a week and occupational therapy four days a week. I was very busy. I had to wear the brace because the bones in my wrist/arm were bent in the wrong position due to lack of use of my right arm. I was doing much better with my ability to swallow and the feeding tube would only be needed for a little longer. It was actually removed the following June, allowing me to eat anything. I still remember how much it hurt to get that feeding tube yanked out. They really just pulled it out; hard, ouch! I still cringe from the memory. I was always quite thin and all the calories I burned just trying to chew prevented me from gaining any weight. I was able to move my tongue more and had more control over my mouth. Before the accident, I loved to draw. I still did and I drew profusely just to relax. I used to be right-handed. I did well transitioning to my left hand. I was also seeing my psychologist, Dr. Irving, on a regular basis and it was very helpful.

The Road Less Traveled

Mom was embarking on a new path in her career. She loved working in Nuclear Medicine at St. John Hospital. She was now taking a faculty position at Macomb Community College where she would teach what she had done for the last twenty years. The remarkable thing about all of this was that the position simply materialized. She didn't know anything about it. It was offered to her. She saw it as an opportunity of a lifetime. She loved to teach. She was sad to be leaving St. John's and all her co-workers, but in the end, she knew she had made the right decision.

Dad had left his job. He concluded that he would look after me full-time. It was a tremendous decision for him and Mom to make, but during the time I was getting stronger and healthier, another position opened at the college. Mom informed Dad of it as she knew he possessed all of the qualifications it required. After several interviews, he was hired. It was just what he loved to do in computer web-design.

Dad was also presented with the opportunity to advance his education. He already had a Bachelor's Degree in Business Administration. One of his proudest moments was when he graduated with another degree at the college pertaining to web-design. He beamed as he crossed that stage to receive his diploma where Mom was one of the members of the faculty who shook his hand.

It really did seem as though a higher power was looking after my parents as they were looking after me.

The Choice Was Mine

Many people have been intrigued by the account of my after-death experience. I don't feel the need to convince anyone of its authenticity. I just know that the memory of it is as striking today as when it happened. I am now eighteen years old and in my senior year in high school. The content of my story has not changed. I am just better at sharing it now. I've grown and matured. I have become better educated and more able to articulate the event which I remember vividly; with a clarity and emotion that is not a part of our world.

In 2013 I partook in a study for The Near-Death Experience Foundation, conducted by scientists. It was begun by Dr. Jeffrey Long, author of the book, Evidence of the Afterlife. He is a physician, practicing the specialty of radiation oncology (use of radiation to treat cancer) in Houston, Louisiana. Dr. Long served on the Board of Directors of IANDS (International Association for Near-Death Studies) and is actively involved in NDE research. After the study, it was determined that my experience was valid.

One of the questions asked was whether or not my values or beliefs had changed after the experience. I know I have changed. I have a much closer relationship with God. I now tend to befriend other people more. About five years after my accident, I told my mom that I was glad it had happened. She just looked at me incredulously and asked why! I simply responded that I wasn't such a nice person before and since that time, I had become a better person.

My sister Lily won a scholarship to Wayne State University after graduation from high school and is pursuing a degree in social work. She also wants to go to law school. My brother Erik is now in Macomb College and has been active in theater. He has been in some wonderful musicals with a company called All the World's a Stage. We even went to Disneyworld in Florida where he was appearing with the other actors, selected to intern, and will be performing in the Park for the next few months. However, Erik wants to become a teacher like Mom, only he wants to teach high school students. We have come a long way since my accident. My siblings were traumatized by the event and needed counseling. I do not want them to bear the effects of what happened.   It was an accident; and it's over.

The high school I attend in Warren is about a mile and a half from where Nana and Poppy live. It is the same school my brother and sister attended and my parents, Michael and Sharon, attended. Mom and Dad and Lily and Erik all take turns getting me to and from school. Sometimes I will walk over to Nana and Poppy's house and sometimes Nana will pick me up.   I have continued my therapy at Children's Hospital in Detroit although I have had much less of it in the past two years.

Meals are much easier for me now and I try to have them all the time, one after the other, as often as possible. I'm still very thin but I have a ravenous appetite and love to eat! I can talk now, but with some difficulty. I'm using my left hand skillfully even with some of its limitations. My right hand is not as strong as my left.

I love school and I especially love drawing. I am a member of the National Technical Honor Society and have a high GPA   I want a career as a sequential (aka comic book) artist and I'm looking forward to pursuing my dream.   I am currently deciding on which college to go to, and so far, I have been accepted and received scholarships to my "dream" colleges; including Savannah College of Art and Design, Minneapolis College of Art and Design, and College for Creative Studies, in Detroit. I spent three weeks in Minneapolis (on my own, living in the dorm) and took some college courses. I loved it and learned a lot. I am also enrolled in college courses at Macomb Community College while finishing high school.

I was in band at school, playing the cymbals and drums. I even marched in the Thanksgiving Day Parade in downtown Detroit. I love to read poetry and books about history, current events and politics. I'm also teaching myself to speak Japanese and am pretty good at it.

Vault of Heaven

I like to share my thoughts with Nana and Poppy about the things I'm learning and Nana likes to read my school books. One afternoon at their house, I asked Nana what she knew about Adolf Hitler. We were learning about World War II and were aghast at the evil, cruel and sadistic events which took place as a result of his villainy; where millions lost their lives and untold suffering plagued the planet. I also asked Nana if she thought Hitler knew the difference between right and wrong. I come from a Catholic family. Even if we didn't come from any religious background, certainly we would still know right from wrong and good from evil! Hitler was a Catholic. Did he ever learn anything about God? I wondered; if he had repented, could he possibly be in Heaven? I wondered about justice.

Nana prefaced what she was going to say with "Coriander, (she still calls me Coriander) no one really knows what happens after we die," to which I quickly interjected a resounding, "I do!" She smiled and said she guessed I did.

I was telling Nana and Poppy that sometimes I become very annoyed with some of my classmates. There are various reasons as to why. I said I even want to respond to them with meanness, but I can hear Jesus tell me that I have to be kind. Poppy said I was referring to my conscience. We all have one. Nana agreed. I left it at that. I know what I'm hearing. Kindness to one another is what Jesus expects. It makes the world a better place. Kindness is found in the vault of Heaven. Everyone is important to God.

"That's Him!"   The Shroud of Turin

Mom and I were watching a documentary on television about the *Shroud of Turin*. Up until that time, I had never heard of the shroud. It was kept in Turin, Italy and was believed by some to be the burial cloth of Jesus of Nazareth.   The details of the shroud are not entirely visible to the naked eye and were first observed after the advent of photography in the 1890's.   There appeared a startling image on the negative.   It was of a man who had suffered physical trauma consistent with crucifixion. Since that time, as modern technology developed, more tests were conducted on the cloth.

I watched the documentary in fascination as scientists were explaining the computerized three dimensional technique; capable of lifting the details from the cloth into an actual human form. I have seen many artist renditions of the image of Jesus. In some he appears as a blue-eyed blonde baby. Others portray Jesus as a child with long brown hair and brown eyes.   Still others show him to be a gentle young man with smooth skin and perfect features.

I've seen portraits of Jesus on the cross, only to emerge gloriously after his resurrection. He has also been portrayed as a rugged individual with Mid-Eastern features or someone with very dark skin and curly hair. None of these pictures have ever made much of an impression on me because I knew no one could possibly know how Jesus looked, save for the real or imagined typical appearance of a Jewish man living in the ancient Mid-Eastern world.

I was not prepared for my reaction when I saw the three dimensional face of the man lifted off the shroud, simulating what he may have looked like in life. The eyes were closed, after which, they opened.

I knew him. I was not experiencing a recollection. It was a definite recognition. This image evoked the sense of familiarity I experienced while I had been in Heaven. Mom watched me move to the edge of my seat as I quietly said, "It's Him."

A day or two later, I was visiting with Nana and asked her if she ever saw anything about the shroud. She said she remembered first learning of it as a child, watching a program about it on black and white television. Since then she had acquired more information about it. She had seen the same documentary that Mom and I had and thought it quite amazing. She went on to say she would like to believe it's true. Since so much of it reflects the wounds of Jesus described in the Gospels, it would be a beautiful gift preserved by the ancient world, bequeathed to the modern world, and intended to be carefully unwrapped by the development of the technology of the nineteenth, twentieth and twenty-first centuries. It would appear to her as a deliberate means of God breaking into the modern world.

Mom walked into Nana's house and asked her if I had told her of my reaction while watching the documentary on the *Shroud of Turin*. Nana looked at me quizzically and said that I hadn't. Mom said, "That's Him! Corey said, 'that's Him!'" All three of us smiled.

The Lady in the Rocking Chair

As usual, I was sitting at Nana's kitchen table scarfing down everything she placed in front of me. She started to tell me that she sometimes laughs at some of the antics I pulled while I was hospitalized after my accident. She especially thought my temper tantrum, kicking my tray table out of the room, and rolling my nourishment cans down the hall because I had to wear a tether to contain me was comical. It became more so when the very large security guard asked "if there was a problem" and I withered away from him, never to be heard from again until morning. I said I had "no memory of it at all." She was surprised to hear that because it happened shortly before I was released from the hospital. I continued that I could only put together bits and pieces of those weeks. I could remember beds, hallways, medical personnel and bizarre dreams of super heroes and Sesame Street.

The only thing I remembered with clarity was my sitter. Nana asked what I meant. She said I didn't have a sitter. I replied that she must remember the lady in the rocking chair who always sat with me. Nana said there was no sitter and there never was a rocker in any of the rooms I was in. I said I vividly remembered a lady who watched me constantly. She moved with me from room to room. She sometimes looked worried and concerned, but most of the time she smiled; enjoying just being with me. She was kindly. I went on to describe her. I said she had a look about her as though she were a schoolteacher. She was elderly, wore glasses, and piled her hair in a bun high up on her head. Nana said that description fit her grandmother.

We looked at very old pictures. Nana asked me to go through them. From the photos, I *found* my great-great grandmother and *recognized* her as the "lady in the rocking chair." I thought it was kind of spooky. Nana said that was nonsense. It was beautiful! She went on to say that it would be just like her Babcia, caring for her family; even from Heaven.

It's unfortunate that I never mentioned this while my great grandmother, Busia, was alive. Busia would have liked to have known that her mother was still baby-sitting. She also would have enjoyed hearing that I saw her daughter, Helen, float out of her wheelchair. Nana and I both smiled because we knew Busia was certainly aware of it now.

The Heaven Experience

I have been given a glimpse of Heaven. I am honored and humbled to have made the same extraordinary journey as countless others. For me, it was the result of an accident.

Up until now, I didn't realize the agony and suffering my drowning caused my family and friends; and that saddens me. I didn't really think about my frantic mother, my guilt-ridden father and my horror-stricken brother and sister. I was a child then and I thought as a child. My family is aware of my conviction that I had the privilege of being present with God and my deceased relatives in Heaven, along with being forever grateful and truly blessed. I'm content and happy and just love life. My eyes always seem to be smiling.

I want nothing but good things for everyone, for we are all connected. I truly believe we should always hope and have faith at all times.

If I were to sum it all together, I would suggest we listen to Jesus. He said we should "love one another." I will never be able to express the magnitude of the love found in Heaven. In this life's journey, we can replicate it somewhat by being kind to one another. This is how we love and honor God.

With that in mind, we *experience* Heaven; for Heaven is within each of us.

You're Here
to Corey

What brought you back
From the other side?
You were there, you know.
You left us.
What brought you back,
or should we ask
who brought you back?
We know you were there
and we know
who is there.
Your return is no accident
no coincidence.
You are here because of...

Justine E. Peña
A Few More Thoughts
© 2012

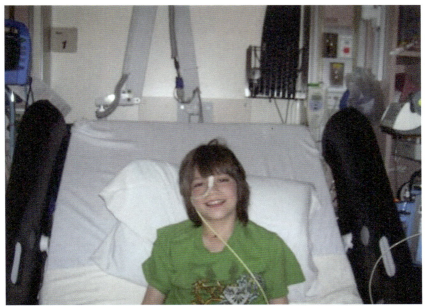

Corey at C. S. Mott Children's Hospital - Ann Arbor, MI - July 2007

In the Play Area at Mott Hospital - Ann Arbor, MI

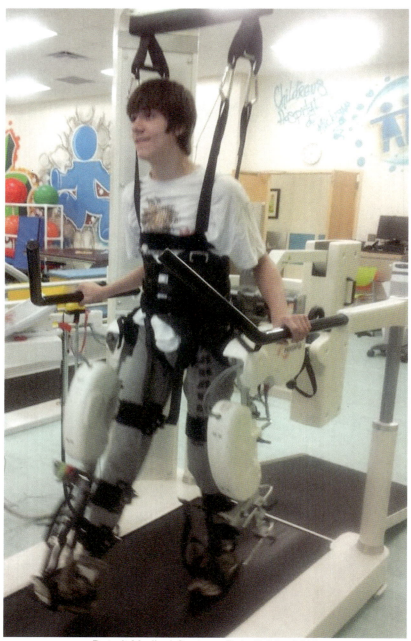

Detroit Medical Center – Detroit, MI - 2013